READERS FOR TEENS

Twelve Things to Do at Age 12

Marcia Wuest

Series coordinator
Sérgio Varela

CAMBRIDGE UNIVERSITY PRESS
Cambridge, New York, Melbourne, Madrid, Cape Town, Singapore, São Paulo, Delhi

Cambridge University Press
32 Avenue of the Americas, New York 10013-2473, USA

www.cambridge.org/elt/readersforteens/

© Cambridge University Press 2009

This publication is in copyright. Subject to statutory exception
and to the provisions of relevant collective licensing agreements,
no reproduction of any part may take place without the written
permission of Cambridge University Press.

First published 2009

Printed in Hong Kong, China, by Golden Cup Printing Limited

ISBN 978-0-521-73733-3 paperback (English)
ISBN 978-0-521-73734-0 paperback (Portuguese)

Cambridge University Press has no responsibility for
the persistence or accuracy of URLs for external or
third-party Internet Web sites referred to in this publication,
and does not guarantee that any content on such
Web sites is, or will remain, accurate or appropriate.

Illustrations by Amilcar Pinna

Art direction, book design, and layout services: A+ Comunicação, Brazil

Contents

Chapter 1
Tomorrow is my birthday.　　5

Chapter 2
Dog treats　　9

Chapter 3
Birthday presents　　13

Chapter 4
The list　　18

Chapter 5
Thirteen things to do at age 13　　20

Chapter 1
Tomorrow is my birthday.

My alarm clock is ringing. It's Saturday, but I can't sleep late today. I have a lot of things to do. First, I need to find my notebook.

I get up and look around. Where's my notebook? Ah! There it is – on the desk, under my laptop. I get it, then sit down on my bed and read my list: *Twelve Things to Do at Age 12*.

My phone rings, and I answer it.

"Hello," I say.

It's my 20-year-old brother, Paco.

"Hey, Diego! It's your 13th birthday tomorrow," says Paco. "Are you excited?"

"I am, but . . ." Paco wants to see my list of *Twelve Things to Do at Age 12*.

"Can we go for ice cream this afternoon?" he asks.

"Hmm," I think. I don't want Paco to look at my list. There are only 11 checks on it – I still have one last thing to do. I don't want to tell Paco this.

Twelve Things to Do at Age 12
By Diego

1. Go biking two days a week. ✓
2. Go camping with Paco. ✓
3. Eat healthy snacks. ✓
4. Do extra science homework. ✓
5. Study with my friends every weekend. ✓
6. Read 10 books. ✓
7. Play tennis every Friday. ✓
8. Make a surprise breakfast for Mom and Dad. ✓
9. Learn to cook. ✓
10. Visit Grandma every week. ✓
11. Collect trash on the beach. ✓
12. Help someone not in my family.

"Well . . ." I start, but I hear a noise outside. I look out of my window. Next door, Emma, my neighbor, and Hee Soon, her best friend, are chasing a small dog. But the puppy isn't playing – it's running away.

"Come here!" the girls shout, but the puppy doesn't listen. It runs into the garage and out again. Emma and Hee Soon follow the puppy. It's like a circus, but it isn't funny.

Now the puppy runs out of the yard. The girls are worried.

"Hmm," I think. "Emma doesn't have a puppy." I can hear them shouting, "Stop! Stop!" on the street in front of my house. Maybe they need help.

"Paco, can I call you later?" I ask. "I think my neighbor has a problem."

"Sure," he says.

I change into a T-shirt, shorts, and sneakers, and run out of the house.

Chapter 2
Dog treats

Emma and Hee Soon are now chasing the puppy from yard to yard. The girls are tired. Emma shouts again. The puppy doesn't pay any attention and runs into the street near the bus stop. It's dangerous.

"Oh, no!" screams Emma. She sees me and says, "Please get my puppy, Diego!" Emma's puppy runs down the street.

"I can try. What's the puppy's name?" I ask.

"He, um… he doesn't have a name," Emma says.

"Yeah. He's Emma's early birthday present," says Hee Soon.

I think for a minute. I know! Dog treats. My dog does *anything* for a dog treat. Maybe Emma's puppy likes treats, too.

"Stay here – I have an idea," I say. I hurry home for some dog treats.

A few minutes later, I'm back with the treats. But Emma and Hee Soon aren't there. "Oh, no! Where are they now?"

I look down the street – Emma's puppy is running toward the park. Emma and Hee Soon are running, too. The puppy is fast. They can't catch him. A car is coming. Emma is very upset. The car slows down.

I run. "Please stay there, puppy," I think.

The puppy stops running and watches me – he's quiet. The car goes by. Good! Then the puppy hears a sound – and runs again.

"Here." I hold out a treat. The puppy stops and looks around.

"Eat the treat!" I say. And he eats it. I'm happy. I put a second treat in my hand.

"Good boy. Come and get the treat!" I say. The puppy eats the second treat.

Chapter 3
Birthday presents

Emma puts the leash on the puppy. He can't run now.

"Thank you, Diego!" Emma is so happy. "Thank you for getting my birthday present back!" Emma is hugging her cute puppy.

"No problem," I say. "So, when's your birthday?"

"Tomorrow," Emma says.

"*Really?*" I'm surprised. "My birthday is tomorrow, too."

"No kidding!" says Emma. "Yeah, it's my 13th birthday."

"Yeah? Me too," I say. "And thank you for my great birthday present."

Emma and Hee Soon look at each other. They don't understand.

"What present?" asks Hee Soon.

"Come to my house, and you can see it," I say to Emma and Hee Soon.

We walk home together. Emma's puppy doesn't like the leash and pulls hard.

"Walk!" says Emma. "I want to teach him, but . . ."

"Here, use the treats," I say. She gives him a treat. It's a good idea, and the puppy walks.

Inside my house, I run to my room and get my notebook. In the living room, Emma, Hee Soon, and Emma's puppy are waiting with my dog, Charlie. He's a big dog, but her puppy likes him. He wants to play.

"Here," I say, and I open my notebook to my list of *Twelve Things to Do at Age 12*.

I give it to Emma and Hee Soon, and they read my list.

6. Read 10 books. ✓ ... every weekend. ✓
7. Play tennis every Friday. ✓
8. Make a surprise breakfast for Mom and D...
9. Learn to cook. ✓
10. Visit Grandma every week. ✓
11. Collect trash on the beach. ✓
12. Help someone not in my family.

Hee Soon and Emma still don't understand. "Is this list your birthday present?" Hee Soon asks.

"No. But look at the last thing on the list," I say.

Emma reads, "Help someone not in my family."

"See?" I say. "Because of you and your puppy, my list is finished now."

"Oh, I see," says Emma. "That's great."

"I'm so happy. Thank you!" I say.

"Can I put a check next to number 12 on the list then?" asks Emma.

"Sure," I say. And I give her a pencil.

Chapter 4
The list

Charlie and I walk with Emma, Hee Soon, and the puppy to Emma's house.

"Diego, I like your list of *Twelve Things to Do at Age 12*. It's a great idea," says Hee Soon. "Do you make one every year?"

"Yes," I say. "Every year on our birthdays, my brother, Paco, and I make a list of things we want to do that year."

"And are the number of things on the list and your age the same?" asks Emma.

"Yes," I say. "So, tomorrow I need a list with 13 things on it!"

"Cool!" says Emma.

"Yeah," I say. "Now, Paco can read my list of *Twelve Things to Do at Age 12*."

I *really* want Paco to read it because he leaves for art school in France next week. "Study in France" is number 16 on his list of *Twenty Things to Do at Age 20*.

"Paco isn't just my brother – he's my best friend, too," I tell the girls.

"That's nice," says Hee Soon. "Family and friends are really important. We can all help each other."

"Yes, we can," Emma says.

"Do you both want to make a list of *Thirteen Things to Do at Age 13?*" I ask.

"Yes. Great idea!" they say.

"The first thing on my list is *name the puppy!*" Emma laughs.

I leave Emma's house and call Paco. I have time for ice cream now.

Chapter 5
Thirteen things to do at age 13

The next morning, I hear Emma and Hee Soon at the kitchen door.

"Happy birthday!" the girls shout.

"You too, Emma!" I say.

"Look! I have my list. Can you read it?" Emma asks. "What do you think?"

I read Emma's list of *Thirteen Things to Do at Age 13*. There's already a check next to number one – "Name the puppy." I smile.

"This is a great list," I say.

"So, what's your name?" I hold my hand out to Emma's puppy. He's looking for another treat. I give him one.

"His name is Treat," Emma says. "He loves those treats – and does anything for one. Well, you know that!"

"Oh, it's a great name for him," I say.

"I have a list, too," Hee Soon says. "Can you read it, too?"

"Sure," I say. We sit at the kitchen table.

I read Hee Soon's list. The first thing it says is: "Be Diego's friend."

"We know Paco leaves soon. So, we want you to hang out with us," says Hee Soon.

"I'd really like that," I tell them.

What a great birthday! I have checks next to everything on my list of *Twelve Things to Do at Age 12 – and* I have two new friends. Oh, wait! I have three. Treat is also my new friend.

"Here!" says Hee Soon. "I have a birthday cake for you and Emma. Let's eat."

"And here are some treats for Treat and Charlie," says Emma.

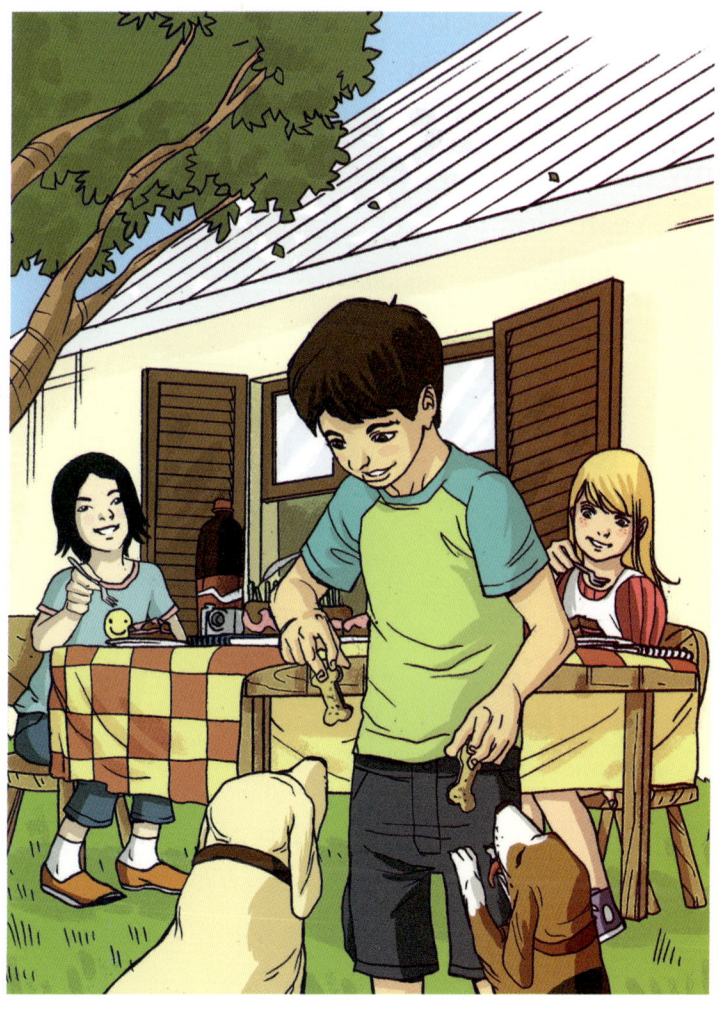

I'm very lucky.

"Let's take a photo for Paco," Emma says. We take a picture of me with my three new friends and Charlie.

"You can give the photo and a copy of your *new* list to Paco," says Hee Soon.

"Oh, that's right!" I say. "I want to give Paco my list of *Thirteen Things to Do at Age 13*."

"Yeah, don't forget that!" says Emma. And we all laugh.